50 Turkish Delights
Recipes for Home

By: Kelly Johnson

Table of Contents

- Classic Rose-flavored Turkish Delight
- Pistachio Turkish Delight
- Orange and Almond Turkish Delight
- Lemon Turkish Delight
- Mint Turkish Delight
- Hazelnut Turkish Delight
- Raspberry Turkish Delight
- Coconut Turkish Delight
- Coffee Turkish Delight
- Vanilla Turkish Delight
- Pomegranate Turkish Delight
- Chocolate Turkish Delight
- Cardamom Turkish Delight
- Honey Turkish Delight
- Saffron Turkish Delight
- Walnut Turkish Delight
- Apple Turkish Delight
- Cherry Turkish Delight
- Apricot Turkish Delight
- Blackberry Turkish Delight
- Mango Turkish Delight
- Pineapple Turkish Delight
- Cranberry Turkish Delight
- Ginger Turkish Delight
- Cinnamon Turkish Delight
- Blueberry Turkish Delight
- Elderflower Turkish Delight
- Lavender Turkish Delight
- Anise Turkish Delight
- Rosemary Turkish Delight
- Fig Turkish Delight
- Date Turkish Delight
- Mulberry Turkish Delight
- Tamarind Turkish Delight
- Grape Turkish Delight
- Plum Turkish Delight

- Lychee Turkish Delight
- Passionfruit Turkish Delight
- Kiwi Turkish Delight
- Guava Turkish Delight
- Watermelon Turkish Delight
- Papaya Turkish Delight
- Pear Turkish Delight
- Quince Turkish Delight
- Nectarine Turkish Delight
- Persimmon Turkish Delight
- Caramel Turkish Delight
- Pistachio-Rose Turkish Delight
- Orange Blossom Turkish Delight
- Blackcurrant Turkish Delight

Classic Rose-flavored Turkish Delight

Ingredients:

- 2 cups granulated sugar
- 1 cup water
- 1 tablespoon lemon juice
- 1 cup cornstarch
- 1 1/2 cups water
- 1 tablespoon rose water
- Red food coloring (optional)

Instructions:

1. Grease a square baking dish (about 8x8 inches) with oil and line it with parchment paper. This will make it easier to remove the Turkish delight once it sets.
2. In a medium saucepan, combine the sugar, 1 cup of water, and lemon juice. Stir over medium heat until the sugar dissolves completely.
3. In a separate bowl, mix the cornstarch with 1 1/2 cups of water until smooth and there are no lumps.
4. Gradually pour the cornstarch mixture into the saucepan with the sugar syrup, stirring constantly to prevent lumps from forming.
5. Cook the mixture over medium heat, stirring frequently, until it thickens and starts to pull away from the sides of the pan. This can take about 15-20 minutes.
6. Stir in the rose water and add a few drops of red food coloring if desired, to achieve a light pink color. Mix well.
7. Continue to cook the mixture for another 5-10 minutes until it becomes very thick and glossy.
8. Immediately pour the hot mixture into the prepared baking dish. Smooth out the top with an oiled spatula or spoon.
9. Allow the Turkish delight to cool at room temperature for several hours, until it is completely set and firm.
10. Once set, lift the Turkish delight out of the baking dish using the parchment paper. Place it on a cutting board and cut it into small squares or rectangles using a sharp knife.
11. Dust the cut pieces with powdered sugar to prevent them from sticking together.
12. Your Classic Rose-flavored Turkish Delight is now ready to be enjoyed! Store the pieces in an airtight container at room temperature for up to two weeks.

Pistachio Turkish Delight

Ingredients:

- 2 cups granulated sugar
- 1 cup water
- 1 tablespoon lemon juice
- 1 cup cornstarch
- 1 1/2 cups water
- 1 tablespoon rose water
- 1/2 cup shelled pistachios, chopped
- Green food coloring (optional)

Instructions:

1. Prepare a square baking dish (about 8x8 inches) by greasing it with oil and lining it with parchment paper.
2. In a medium saucepan, combine the sugar, 1 cup of water, and lemon juice. Stir over medium heat until the sugar dissolves completely.
3. In a separate bowl, mix the cornstarch with 1 1/2 cups of water until smooth and there are no lumps.
4. Gradually pour the cornstarch mixture into the saucepan with the sugar syrup, stirring constantly to prevent lumps.
5. Cook the mixture over medium heat, stirring frequently, until it thickens and starts to pull away from the sides of the pan. This can take about 15-20 minutes.
6. Stir in the rose water and chopped pistachios. Add a few drops of green food coloring if desired, to enhance the pistachio color. Mix well.
7. Continue to cook the mixture for another 5-10 minutes until it becomes very thick and glossy.
8. Immediately pour the hot mixture into the prepared baking dish. Smooth out the top with an oiled spatula or spoon.
9. Allow the Turkish delight to cool at room temperature for several hours, until it is completely set and firm.
10. Once set, lift the Turkish delight out of the baking dish using the parchment paper. Place it on a cutting board and cut it into small squares or rectangles using a sharp knife.
11. Dust the cut pieces with powdered sugar to prevent them from sticking together.
12. Your Pistachio Turkish Delight is now ready to be enjoyed! Store the pieces in an airtight container at room temperature for up to two weeks.

Enjoy your homemade Pistachio Turkish Delight!

Orange and Almond Turkish Delight

Ingredients:

- 2 cups granulated sugar
- 1 cup water
- 1 tablespoon lemon juice
- 1 cup cornstarch
- 1 1/2 cups water
- 1 tablespoon orange blossom water
- Zest of 1 orange
- 1/2 cup almonds, finely chopped
- Orange food coloring (optional)

Instructions:

1. Prepare a square baking dish (about 8x8 inches) by greasing it with oil and lining it with parchment paper.
2. In a medium saucepan, combine the sugar, 1 cup of water, and lemon juice. Stir over medium heat until the sugar dissolves completely.
3. In a separate bowl, mix the cornstarch with 1 1/2 cups of water until smooth and there are no lumps.
4. Gradually pour the cornstarch mixture into the saucepan with the sugar syrup, stirring constantly to prevent lumps.
5. Cook the mixture over medium heat, stirring frequently, until it thickens and starts to pull away from the sides of the pan. This can take about 15-20 minutes.
6. Stir in the orange blossom water, orange zest, and chopped almonds. Add a few drops of orange food coloring if desired, to enhance the orange color. Mix well.
7. Continue to cook the mixture for another 5-10 minutes until it becomes very thick and glossy.
8. Immediately pour the hot mixture into the prepared baking dish. Smooth out the top with an oiled spatula or spoon.
9. Allow the Turkish delight to cool at room temperature for several hours, until it is completely set and firm.
10. Once set, lift the Turkish delight out of the baking dish using the parchment paper. Place it on a cutting board and cut it into small squares or rectangles using a sharp knife.
11. Dust the cut pieces with powdered sugar to prevent them from sticking together.
12. Your Orange and Almond Turkish Delight is now ready to be enjoyed! Store the pieces in an airtight container at room temperature for up to two weeks.

Enjoy the delightful combination of orange zest and almonds in this Turkish delight!

Lemon Turkish Delight

Ingredients:

- 2 cups granulated sugar
- 1 cup water
- 1 tablespoon lemon juice
- Zest of 1 lemon
- 1 cup cornstarch
- 1 1/2 cups water
- Yellow food coloring (optional)
- Powdered sugar, for dusting

Instructions:

1. Grease a square baking dish (about 8x8 inches) with oil and line it with parchment paper.
2. In a medium saucepan, combine the sugar, 1 cup of water, lemon juice, and lemon zest. Stir over medium heat until the sugar dissolves completely.
3. In a separate bowl, mix the cornstarch with 1 1/2 cups of water until smooth and there are no lumps.
4. Gradually pour the cornstarch mixture into the saucepan with the sugar syrup, stirring constantly to prevent lumps.
5. Cook the mixture over medium heat, stirring frequently, until it thickens and starts to pull away from the sides of the pan. This can take about 15-20 minutes.
6. If using, add a few drops of yellow food coloring to achieve a lemony color. Mix well.
7. Continue to cook the mixture for another 5-10 minutes until it becomes very thick and glossy.
8. Immediately pour the hot mixture into the prepared baking dish. Smooth out the top with an oiled spatula or spoon.
9. Allow the Turkish delight to cool at room temperature for several hours, until it is completely set and firm.
10. Once set, lift the Turkish delight out of the baking dish using the parchment paper. Place it on a cutting board and cut it into small squares or rectangles using a sharp knife.
11. Dust the cut pieces with powdered sugar to prevent them from sticking together.
12. Your Lemon Turkish Delight is now ready to be enjoyed! Store the pieces in an airtight container at room temperature for up to two weeks.

This lemon-flavored Turkish delight is refreshing and delightful with its citrusy aroma and flavor. Enjoy making and sharing this sweet treat!

Mint Turkish Delight

Ingredients:

- 2 cups granulated sugar
- 1 cup water
- 1 tablespoon lemon juice
- 1 cup cornstarch
- 1 1/2 cups water
- 1/2 teaspoon peppermint extract
- Green food coloring (optional)
- Powdered sugar, for dusting

Instructions:

1. Grease a square baking dish (about 8x8 inches) with oil and line it with parchment paper.
2. In a medium saucepan, combine the sugar, 1 cup of water, and lemon juice. Stir over medium heat until the sugar dissolves completely.
3. In a separate bowl, mix the cornstarch with 1 1/2 cups of water until smooth and there are no lumps.
4. Gradually pour the cornstarch mixture into the saucepan with the sugar syrup, stirring constantly to prevent lumps.
5. Cook the mixture over medium heat, stirring frequently, until it thickens and starts to pull away from the sides of the pan. This can take about 15-20 minutes.
6. Stir in the peppermint extract and add a few drops of green food coloring if desired, to achieve a minty color. Mix well.
7. Continue to cook the mixture for another 5-10 minutes until it becomes very thick and glossy.
8. Immediately pour the hot mixture into the prepared baking dish. Smooth out the top with an oiled spatula or spoon.
9. Allow the Turkish delight to cool at room temperature for several hours, until it is completely set and firm.
10. Once set, lift the Turkish delight out of the baking dish using the parchment paper. Place it on a cutting board and cut it into small squares or rectangles using a sharp knife.
11. Dust the cut pieces with powdered sugar to prevent them from sticking together.
12. Your Mint Turkish Delight is now ready to be enjoyed! Store the pieces in an airtight container at room temperature for up to two weeks.

This mint-flavored Turkish delight offers a refreshing twist on the classic recipe, perfect for mint lovers!

Hazelnut Turkish Delight

Ingredients:

- 2 cups granulated sugar
- 1 cup water
- 1 tablespoon lemon juice
- 1 cup cornstarch
- 1 1/2 cups water
- 1 teaspoon hazelnut extract
- 1/2 cup hazelnuts, toasted and chopped
- Brown food coloring (optional)
- Powdered sugar, for dusting

Instructions:

1. Grease a square baking dish (about 8x8 inches) with oil and line it with parchment paper.
2. In a medium saucepan, combine the sugar, 1 cup of water, and lemon juice. Stir over medium heat until the sugar dissolves completely.
3. In a separate bowl, mix the cornstarch with 1 1/2 cups of water until smooth and there are no lumps.
4. Gradually pour the cornstarch mixture into the saucepan with the sugar syrup, stirring constantly to prevent lumps.
5. Cook the mixture over medium heat, stirring frequently, until it thickens and starts to pull away from the sides of the pan. This can take about 15-20 minutes.
6. Stir in the hazelnut extract and chopped hazelnuts. Add a few drops of brown food coloring if desired, to enhance the hazelnut color. Mix well.
7. Continue to cook the mixture for another 5-10 minutes until it becomes very thick and glossy.
8. Immediately pour the hot mixture into the prepared baking dish. Smooth out the top with an oiled spatula or spoon.
9. Allow the Turkish delight to cool at room temperature for several hours, until it is completely set and firm.
10. Once set, lift the Turkish delight out of the baking dish using the parchment paper. Place it on a cutting board and cut it into small squares or rectangles using a sharp knife.
11. Dust the cut pieces with powdered sugar to prevent them from sticking together.
12. Your Hazelnut Turkish Delight is now ready to be enjoyed! Store the pieces in an airtight container at room temperature for up to two weeks.

This hazelnut-flavored Turkish delight is rich with the nutty aroma and crunch of toasted hazelnuts, making it a delightful treat for any occasion. Enjoy making and sharing this delicious confection!

Raspberry Turkish Delight

Ingredients:

- 2 cups granulated sugar
- 1 cup water
- 1 tablespoon lemon juice
- 1 cup cornstarch
- 1 1/2 cups water
- 1/2 cup raspberry juice (freshly squeezed or store-bought)
- Red food coloring (optional)
- Powdered sugar, for dusting

Instructions:

1. Grease a square baking dish (about 8x8 inches) with oil and line it with parchment paper.
2. In a medium saucepan, combine the sugar, 1 cup of water, and lemon juice. Stir over medium heat until the sugar dissolves completely.
3. In a separate bowl, mix the cornstarch with 1 1/2 cups of water until smooth and there are no lumps.
4. Gradually pour the cornstarch mixture into the saucepan with the sugar syrup, stirring constantly to prevent lumps.
5. Cook the mixture over medium heat, stirring frequently, until it thickens and starts to pull away from the sides of the pan. This can take about 15-20 minutes.
6. Stir in the raspberry juice and add a few drops of red food coloring if desired, to enhance the raspberry color. Mix well.
7. Continue to cook the mixture for another 5-10 minutes until it becomes very thick and glossy.
8. Immediately pour the hot mixture into the prepared baking dish. Smooth out the top with an oiled spatula or spoon.
9. Allow the Turkish delight to cool at room temperature for several hours, until it is completely set and firm.
10. Once set, lift the Turkish delight out of the baking dish using the parchment paper. Place it on a cutting board and cut it into small squares or rectangles using a sharp knife.
11. Dust the cut pieces with powdered sugar to prevent them from sticking together.
12. Your Raspberry Turkish Delight is now ready to be enjoyed! Store the pieces in an airtight container at room temperature for up to two weeks.

This raspberry-flavored Turkish delight is fruity and vibrant, perfect for those who enjoy the tart sweetness of raspberries. Enjoy making and savoring this delightful treat!

Coconut Turkish Delight

Ingredients:

- 2 cups granulated sugar

- 1 cup water
- 1 tablespoon lemon juice
- 1 cup cornstarch
- 1 1/2 cups water
- 1 cup shredded coconut (unsweetened)
- 1 teaspoon coconut extract
- Powdered sugar, for dusting

Instructions:

1. Grease a square baking dish (about 8x8 inches) with oil and line it with parchment paper.
2. In a medium saucepan, combine the sugar, 1 cup of water, and lemon juice. Stir over medium heat until the sugar dissolves completely.
3. In a separate bowl, mix the cornstarch with 1 1/2 cups of water until smooth and there are no lumps.
4. Gradually pour the cornstarch mixture into the saucepan with the sugar syrup, stirring constantly to prevent lumps.
5. Cook the mixture over medium heat, stirring frequently, until it thickens and starts to pull away from the sides of the pan. This can take about 15-20 minutes.
6. Stir in the shredded coconut and coconut extract. Mix well.
7. Continue to cook the mixture for another 5-10 minutes until it becomes very thick and glossy.
8. Immediately pour the hot mixture into the prepared baking dish. Smooth out the top with an oiled spatula or spoon.
9. Allow the Turkish delight to cool at room temperature for several hours, until it is completely set and firm.
10. Once set, lift the Turkish delight out of the baking dish using the parchment paper. Place it on a cutting board and cut it into small squares or rectangles using a sharp knife.
11. Dust the cut pieces with powdered sugar to prevent them from sticking together.
12. Your Coconut Turkish Delight is now ready to be enjoyed! Store the pieces in an airtight container at room temperature for up to two weeks.

This Coconut Turkish Delight offers a tropical twist with its coconut flavor and shredded coconut texture. It's a delightful treat that's perfect for coconut lovers!

Coffee Turkish Delight

Ingredients:

- 2 cups granulated sugar
- 1 cup water

- 1 tablespoon lemon juice
- 1 cup cornstarch
- 1 1/2 cups water
- 2 tablespoons instant coffee powder
- Powdered sugar, for dusting

Instructions:

1. Grease a square baking dish (about 8x8 inches) with oil and line it with parchment paper.
2. In a medium saucepan, combine the sugar, 1 cup of water, and lemon juice. Stir over medium heat until the sugar dissolves completely.
3. In a separate bowl, mix the cornstarch with 1 1/2 cups of water until smooth and there are no lumps.
4. Gradually pour the cornstarch mixture into the saucepan with the sugar syrup, stirring constantly to prevent lumps.
5. Dissolve the instant coffee powder in a small amount of hot water to form a smooth paste. Add this coffee paste to the saucepan mixture and stir well.
6. Cook the mixture over medium heat, stirring frequently, until it thickens and starts to pull away from the sides of the pan. This can take about 15-20 minutes.
7. Continue to cook the mixture for another 5-10 minutes until it becomes very thick and glossy.
8. Immediately pour the hot mixture into the prepared baking dish. Smooth out the top with an oiled spatula or spoon.
9. Allow the Turkish delight to cool at room temperature for several hours, until it is completely set and firm.
10. Once set, lift the Turkish delight out of the baking dish using the parchment paper. Place it on a cutting board and cut it into small squares or rectangles using a sharp knife.
11. Dust the cut pieces with powdered sugar to prevent them from sticking together.
12. Your Coffee Turkish Delight is now ready to be enjoyed! Store the pieces in an airtight container at room temperature for up to two weeks.

This Coffee Turkish Delight recipe offers a rich coffee flavor with a delightful chewy texture, making it a perfect treat for coffee enthusiasts. Enjoy making and savoring this unique twist on traditional Turkish delight!

Vanilla Turkish Delight

Ingredients:

- 2 cups granulated sugar
- 1 cup water
- 1 tablespoon lemon juice

- 1 cup cornstarch
- 1 1/2 cups water
- 1 tablespoon vanilla extract
- Powdered sugar, for dusting

Instructions:

1. Grease a square baking dish (about 8x8 inches) with oil and line it with parchment paper.
2. In a medium saucepan, combine the sugar, 1 cup of water, and lemon juice. Stir over medium heat until the sugar dissolves completely.
3. In a separate bowl, mix the cornstarch with 1 1/2 cups of water until smooth and there are no lumps.
4. Gradually pour the cornstarch mixture into the saucepan with the sugar syrup, stirring constantly to prevent lumps.
5. Cook the mixture over medium heat, stirring frequently, until it thickens and starts to pull away from the sides of the pan. This can take about 15-20 minutes.
6. Stir in the vanilla extract. Mix well to incorporate.
7. Continue to cook the mixture for another 5-10 minutes until it becomes very thick and glossy.
8. Immediately pour the hot mixture into the prepared baking dish. Smooth out the top with an oiled spatula or spoon.
9. Allow the Turkish delight to cool at room temperature for several hours, until it is completely set and firm.
10. Once set, lift the Turkish delight out of the baking dish using the parchment paper. Place it on a cutting board and cut it into small squares or rectangles using a sharp knife.
11. Dust the cut pieces with powdered sugar to prevent them from sticking together.
12. Your Vanilla Turkish Delight is now ready to be enjoyed! Store the pieces in an airtight container at room temperature for up to two weeks.

This Vanilla Turkish Delight recipe offers a classic and comforting flavor with a chewy texture, perfect for those who appreciate the subtle sweetness of vanilla. Enjoy making and sharing this delightful treat!

Pomegranate Turkish Delight

Ingredients:

- 2 cups granulated sugar
- 1 cup water
- 1 tablespoon lemon juice
- 1 cup cornstarch

- 1 1/2 cups water
- 1/2 cup pomegranate juice (freshly squeezed or store-bought)
- Red food coloring (optional)
- Powdered sugar, for dusting

Instructions:

1. Grease a square baking dish (about 8x8 inches) with oil and line it with parchment paper.
2. In a medium saucepan, combine the granulated sugar, 1 cup of water, and lemon juice. Stir over medium heat until the sugar dissolves completely.
3. In a separate bowl, mix the cornstarch with 1 1/2 cups of water until smooth and there are no lumps.
4. Gradually pour the cornstarch mixture into the saucepan with the sugar syrup, stirring constantly to prevent lumps.
5. Stir in the pomegranate juice and add a few drops of red food coloring if desired, to enhance the color. Mix well.
6. Cook the mixture over medium heat, stirring frequently, until it thickens and starts to pull away from the sides of the pan. This usually takes about 15-20 minutes.
7. Continue to cook the mixture for another 5-10 minutes until it becomes very thick and glossy.
8. Immediately pour the hot mixture into the prepared baking dish. Smooth out the top with an oiled spatula or spoon.
9. Allow the Turkish delight to cool at room temperature for several hours, until it is completely set and firm.
10. Once set, lift the Turkish delight out of the baking dish using the parchment paper. Place it on a cutting board and cut it into small squares or rectangles using a sharp knife.
11. Dust the cut pieces with powdered sugar to prevent them from sticking together.
12. Your Pomegranate Turkish Delight is now ready to be enjoyed! Store the pieces in an airtight container at room temperature for up to two weeks.

This Pomegranate Turkish Delight recipe offers a delightful combination of sweet and tangy flavors with a chewy texture, making it a wonderful treat for any occasion. Enjoy making and sharing this delicious confection!

Chocolate Turkish Delight

Ingredients:

- 2 cups granulated sugar
- 1 cup water
- 1 tablespoon lemon juice
- 1 cup cornstarch
- 1 1/2 cups water

- 1/2 cup cocoa powder
- Powdered sugar, for dusting

Instructions:

1. Grease a square baking dish (about 8x8 inches) with oil and line it with parchment paper.
2. In a medium saucepan, combine the granulated sugar, 1 cup of water, and lemon juice. Stir over medium heat until the sugar dissolves completely.
3. In a separate bowl, mix the cornstarch with 1 1/2 cups of water until smooth and there are no lumps.
4. Gradually pour the cornstarch mixture into the saucepan with the sugar syrup, stirring constantly to prevent lumps.
5. Add the cocoa powder to the mixture and whisk thoroughly until well combined.
6. Cook the mixture over medium heat, stirring frequently, until it thickens and starts to pull away from the sides of the pan. This usually takes about 15-20 minutes.
7. Continue to cook the mixture for another 5-10 minutes until it becomes very thick and glossy.
8. Immediately pour the hot mixture into the prepared baking dish. Smooth out the top with an oiled spatula or spoon.
9. Allow the Turkish delight to cool at room temperature for several hours, until it is completely set and firm.
10. Once set, lift the Turkish delight out of the baking dish using the parchment paper. Place it on a cutting board and cut it into small squares or rectangles using a sharp knife.
11. Dust the cut pieces with powdered sugar to prevent them from sticking together.
12. Your Chocolate Turkish Delight is now ready to be enjoyed! Store the pieces in an airtight container at room temperature for up to two weeks.

This Chocolate Turkish Delight recipe combines the rich flavor of cocoa with the chewy texture of traditional Turkish delight, creating a delightful treat for chocolate lovers. Enjoy making and savoring this delicious confection!

Cardamom Turkish Delight

Ingredients:

- 2 cups granulated sugar
- 1 cup water
- 1 tablespoon lemon juice
- 1 cup cornstarch
- 1 1/2 cups water
- 1 teaspoon ground cardamom

- Powdered sugar, for dusting

Instructions:

1. Grease a square baking dish (about 8x8 inches) with oil and line it with parchment paper.
2. In a medium saucepan, combine the granulated sugar, 1 cup of water, and lemon juice. Stir over medium heat until the sugar dissolves completely.
3. In a separate bowl, mix the cornstarch with 1 1/2 cups of water until smooth and there are no lumps.
4. Gradually pour the cornstarch mixture into the saucepan with the sugar syrup, stirring constantly to prevent lumps.
5. Stir in the ground cardamom. Mix well to incorporate.
6. Cook the mixture over medium heat, stirring frequently, until it thickens and starts to pull away from the sides of the pan. This usually takes about 15-20 minutes.
7. Continue to cook the mixture for another 5-10 minutes until it becomes very thick and glossy.
8. Immediately pour the hot mixture into the prepared baking dish. Smooth out the top with an oiled spatula or spoon.
9. Allow the Turkish delight to cool at room temperature for several hours, until it is completely set and firm.
10. Once set, lift the Turkish delight out of the baking dish using the parchment paper. Place it on a cutting board and cut it into small squares or rectangles using a sharp knife.
11. Dust the cut pieces with powdered sugar to prevent them from sticking together.
12. Your Cardamom Turkish Delight is now ready to be enjoyed! Store the pieces in an airtight container at room temperature for up to two weeks.

This Cardamom Turkish Delight recipe offers a delightful blend of aromatic cardamom spice with the sweet chewy texture of Turkish delight. It's a unique and exotic treat that's perfect for sharing and enjoying!

Honey Turkish Delight

Ingredients:

- 2 cups granulated sugar
- 1 cup water
- 1 tablespoon lemon juice
- 1 cup cornstarch
- 1 1/2 cups water
- 1/2 cup honey
- 1 teaspoon vanilla extract (optional)

- Powdered sugar, for dusting

Instructions:

1. Grease a square baking dish (about 8x8 inches) with oil and line it with parchment paper.
2. In a medium saucepan, combine the granulated sugar, 1 cup of water, and lemon juice. Stir over medium heat until the sugar dissolves completely.
3. In a separate bowl, mix the cornstarch with 1 1/2 cups of water until smooth and there are no lumps.
4. Gradually pour the cornstarch mixture into the saucepan with the sugar syrup, stirring constantly to prevent lumps.
5. Stir in the honey and vanilla extract (if using). Mix well to incorporate.
6. Cook the mixture over medium heat, stirring frequently, until it thickens and starts to pull away from the sides of the pan. This usually takes about 15-20 minutes.
7. Continue to cook the mixture for another 5-10 minutes until it becomes very thick and glossy.
8. Immediately pour the hot mixture into the prepared baking dish. Smooth out the top with an oiled spatula or spoon.
9. Allow the Turkish delight to cool at room temperature for several hours, until it is completely set and firm.
10. Once set, lift the Turkish delight out of the baking dish using the parchment paper. Place it on a cutting board and cut it into small squares or rectangles using a sharp knife.
11. Dust the cut pieces with powdered sugar to prevent them from sticking together.
12. Your Honey Turkish Delight is now ready to be enjoyed! Store the pieces in an airtight container at room temperature for up to two weeks.

This Honey Turkish Delight recipe offers a natural sweetness and a soft, chewy texture that's enhanced by the subtle flavor of honey. It's a delightful treat that's perfect for enjoying with tea or coffee. Enjoy making and sharing this traditional Turkish confection!

Saffron Turkish Delight

Ingredients:

- 2 cups granulated sugar
- 1 cup water
- 1 tablespoon lemon juice
- 1 cup cornstarch
- 1 1/2 cups water
- A pinch of saffron threads (about 1/4 teaspoon)
- Powdered sugar, for dusting

Instructions:

1. Grease a square baking dish (about 8x8 inches) with oil and line it with parchment paper.
2. In a small bowl, crush the saffron threads with a mortar and pestle. Pour 1 tablespoon of hot water over the crushed saffron threads and let it steep for 5-10 minutes to extract the color and flavor.
3. In a medium saucepan, combine the granulated sugar, 1 cup of water, and lemon juice. Stir over medium heat until the sugar dissolves completely.
4. In a separate bowl, mix the cornstarch with 1 1/2 cups of water until smooth and there are no lumps.
5. Gradually pour the cornstarch mixture into the saucepan with the sugar syrup, stirring constantly to prevent lumps.
6. Strain the saffron-infused water into the saucepan mixture, discarding any solids. Mix well to incorporate the saffron flavor and color into the Turkish delight mixture.
7. Cook the mixture over medium heat, stirring frequently, until it thickens and starts to pull away from the sides of the pan. This usually takes about 15-20 minutes.
8. Continue to cook the mixture for another 5-10 minutes until it becomes very thick and glossy.
9. Immediately pour the hot mixture into the prepared baking dish. Smooth out the top with an oiled spatula or spoon.
10. Allow the Turkish delight to cool at room temperature for several hours, until it is completely set and firm.
11. Once set, lift the Turkish delight out of the baking dish using the parchment paper. Place it on a cutting board and cut it into small squares or rectangles using a sharp knife.
12. Dust the cut pieces with powdered sugar to prevent them from sticking together.
13. Your Saffron Turkish Delight is now ready to be enjoyed! Store the pieces in an airtight container at room temperature for up to two weeks.

This Saffron Turkish Delight recipe captures the luxurious flavor and vibrant color of saffron, making it a delightful and exotic treat. Enjoy making and savoring this unique variation of Turkish delight!

Walnut Turkish Delight

Ingredients:

- 2 cups granulated sugar
- 1 cup water
- 1 tablespoon lemon juice
- 1 cup cornstarch
- 1 1/2 cups water
- 1 cup walnuts, chopped
- Powdered sugar, for dusting

Instructions:

1. Grease a square baking dish (about 8x8 inches) with oil and line it with parchment paper.
2. In a medium saucepan, combine the granulated sugar, 1 cup of water, and lemon juice. Stir over medium heat until the sugar dissolves completely.
3. In a separate bowl, mix the cornstarch with 1 1/2 cups of water until smooth and there are no lumps.
4. Gradually pour the cornstarch mixture into the saucepan with the sugar syrup, stirring constantly to prevent lumps.
5. Cook the mixture over medium heat, stirring frequently, until it thickens and starts to pull away from the sides of the pan. This usually takes about 15-20 minutes.
6. Stir in the chopped walnuts. Mix well to distribute the walnuts evenly throughout the mixture.
7. Continue to cook the mixture for another 5-10 minutes until it becomes very thick and glossy.
8. Immediately pour the hot mixture into the prepared baking dish. Smooth out the top with an oiled spatula or spoon.
9. Allow the Turkish delight to cool at room temperature for several hours, until it is completely set and firm.
10. Once set, lift the Turkish delight out of the baking dish using the parchment paper. Place it on a cutting board and cut it into small squares or rectangles using a sharp knife.
11. Dust the cut pieces with powdered sugar to prevent them from sticking together.
12. Your Walnut Turkish Delight is now ready to be enjoyed! Store the pieces in an airtight container at room temperature for up to two weeks.

This Walnut Turkish Delight recipe combines the chewy texture of traditional Turkish delight with the crunch and nutty flavor of walnuts, creating a delightful treat that's perfect for sharing or gifting. Enjoy making and savoring this delicious confection!

Apple Turkish Delight

Ingredients:

- 2 cups granulated sugar
- 1 cup water
- 1 tablespoon lemon juice
- 1 cup cornstarch
- 1 1/2 cups water
- 1 cup apple juice (freshly squeezed or store-bought)
- 1/2 cup finely chopped dried apple pieces (optional)
- Powdered sugar, for dusting

Instructions:

1. Grease a square baking dish (about 8x8 inches) with oil and line it with parchment paper.
2. In a medium saucepan, combine the granulated sugar, 1 cup of water, and lemon juice. Stir over medium heat until the sugar dissolves completely.
3. In a separate bowl, mix the cornstarch with 1 1/2 cups of water until smooth and there are no lumps.
4. Gradually pour the cornstarch mixture into the saucepan with the sugar syrup, stirring constantly to prevent lumps.
5. Stir in the apple juice and chopped dried apple pieces (if using). Mix well to incorporate.
6. Cook the mixture over medium heat, stirring frequently, until it thickens and starts to pull away from the sides of the pan. This usually takes about 15-20 minutes.
7. Continue to cook the mixture for another 5-10 minutes until it becomes very thick and glossy.
8. Immediately pour the hot mixture into the prepared baking dish. Smooth out the top with an oiled spatula or spoon.
9. Allow the Turkish delight to cool at room temperature for several hours, until it is completely set and firm.
10. Once set, lift the Turkish delight out of the baking dish using the parchment paper. Place it on a cutting board and cut it into small squares or rectangles using a sharp knife.
11. Dust the cut pieces with powdered sugar to prevent them from sticking together.
12. Your Apple Turkish Delight is now ready to be enjoyed! Store the pieces in an airtight container at room temperature for up to two weeks.

This Apple Turkish Delight recipe offers a refreshing apple flavor and a chewy texture, making it a delightful treat that's perfect for any occasion. Enjoy making and sharing this unique variation of Turkish delight!

Cherry Turkish Delight

Ingredients:

- 2 cups granulated sugar
- 1 cup water
- 1 tablespoon lemon juice
- 1 cup cornstarch
- 1 1/2 cups water
- 1/2 cup cherry juice (freshly squeezed or store-bought)
- Red food coloring (optional)
- Powdered sugar, for dusting

Instructions:

1. Grease a square baking dish (about 8x8 inches) with oil and line it with parchment paper.

2. In a medium saucepan, combine the granulated sugar, 1 cup of water, and lemon juice. Stir over medium heat until the sugar dissolves completely.
3. In a separate bowl, mix the cornstarch with 1 1/2 cups of water until smooth and there are no lumps.
4. Gradually pour the cornstarch mixture into the saucepan with the sugar syrup, stirring constantly to prevent lumps.
5. Stir in the cherry juice and add a few drops of red food coloring if desired, to enhance the color. Mix well.
6. Cook the mixture over medium heat, stirring frequently, until it thickens and starts to pull away from the sides of the pan. This usually takes about 15-20 minutes.
7. Continue to cook the mixture for another 5-10 minutes until it becomes very thick and glossy.
8. Immediately pour the hot mixture into the prepared baking dish. Smooth out the top with an oiled spatula or spoon.
9. Allow the Turkish delight to cool at room temperature for several hours, until it is completely set and firm.
10. Once set, lift the Turkish delight out of the baking dish using the parchment paper. Place it on a cutting board and cut it into small squares or rectangles using a sharp knife.
11. Dust the cut pieces with powdered sugar to prevent them from sticking together.
12. Your Cherry Turkish Delight is now ready to be enjoyed! Store the pieces in an airtight container at room temperature for up to two weeks.

This Cherry Turkish Delight recipe offers a delightful blend of sweet cherry flavor with a chewy texture, making it a perfect treat for cherry lovers. Enjoy making and sharing this delicious confection!

Apricot Turkish Delight

Ingredients:

- 2 cups granulated sugar
- 1 cup water
- 1 tablespoon lemon juice
- 1 cup cornstarch
- 1 1/2 cups water
- 1 cup apricot puree (fresh or canned)
- Powdered sugar, for dusting

Instructions:

1. Grease a square baking dish (about 8x8 inches) with oil and line it with parchment paper.
2. In a medium saucepan, combine the granulated sugar, 1 cup of water, and lemon juice. Stir over medium heat until the sugar dissolves completely.

3. In a separate bowl, mix the cornstarch with 1 1/2 cups of water until smooth and there are no lumps.
4. Gradually pour the cornstarch mixture into the saucepan with the sugar syrup, stirring constantly to prevent lumps.
5. Stir in the apricot puree and mix well to combine.
6. Cook the mixture over medium heat, stirring frequently, until it thickens and starts to pull away from the sides of the pan. This usually takes about 15-20 minutes.
7. Continue to cook the mixture for another 5-10 minutes until it becomes very thick and glossy.
8. Immediately pour the hot mixture into the prepared baking dish. Smooth out the top with an oiled spatula or spoon.
9. Allow the Turkish delight to cool at room temperature for several hours, until it is completely set and firm.
10. Once set, lift the Turkish delight out of the baking dish using the parchment paper. Place it on a cutting board and cut it into small squares or rectangles using a sharp knife.
11. Dust the cut pieces with powdered sugar to prevent them from sticking together.
12. Your Apricot Turkish Delight is now ready to be enjoyed! Store the pieces in an airtight container at room temperature for up to two weeks.

This Apricot Turkish Delight recipe offers a wonderful balance of sweetness and tanginess from the apricot puree, creating a unique and delicious treat. Enjoy making and sharing this delightful confection with family and friends!

Blackberry Turkish Delight

Ingredients:

- 2 cups granulated sugar
- 1 cup water
- 1 tablespoon lemon juice
- 1 cup cornstarch
- 1 1/2 cups water
- 1 cup blackberry puree (fresh or frozen)
- Powdered sugar, for dusting

Instructions:

1. Grease a square baking dish (about 8x8 inches) with oil and line it with parchment paper.
2. In a medium saucepan, combine the granulated sugar, 1 cup of water, and lemon juice. Stir over medium heat until the sugar dissolves completely.

3. In a separate bowl, mix the cornstarch with 1 1/2 cups of water until smooth and there are no lumps.
4. Gradually pour the cornstarch mixture into the saucepan with the sugar syrup, stirring constantly to prevent lumps.
5. Stir in the blackberry puree and mix well to combine.
6. Cook the mixture over medium heat, stirring frequently, until it thickens and starts to pull away from the sides of the pan. This usually takes about 15-20 minutes.
7. Continue to cook the mixture for another 5-10 minutes until it becomes very thick and glossy.
8. Immediately pour the hot mixture into the prepared baking dish. Smooth out the top with an oiled spatula or spoon.
9. Allow the Turkish delight to cool at room temperature for several hours, until it is completely set and firm.
10. Once set, lift the Turkish delight out of the baking dish using the parchment paper. Place it on a cutting board and cut it into small squares or rectangles using a sharp knife.
11. Dust the cut pieces with powdered sugar to prevent them from sticking together.
12. Your Blackberry Turkish Delight is now ready to be enjoyed! Store the pieces in an airtight container at room temperature for up to two weeks.

This Blackberry Turkish Delight recipe captures the essence of fresh blackberries with a chewy, sweet texture that makes for a delightful treat. Enjoy making and sharing this delicious confection with loved ones!

Mango Turkish Delight

Ingredients:

- 2 cups granulated sugar
- 1 cup water
- 1 tablespoon lemon juice
- 1 cup cornstarch
- 1 1/2 cups water
- 1 cup mango puree (fresh or canned)
- Yellow or orange food coloring (optional)
- Powdered sugar, for dusting

Instructions:

1. Grease a square baking dish (about 8x8 inches) with oil and line it with parchment paper.
2. In a medium saucepan, combine the granulated sugar, 1 cup of water, and lemon juice. Stir over medium heat until the sugar dissolves completely.

3. In a separate bowl, mix the cornstarch with 1 1/2 cups of water until smooth and there are no lumps.
4. Gradually pour the cornstarch mixture into the saucepan with the sugar syrup, stirring constantly to prevent lumps.
5. Stir in the mango puree and add a few drops of yellow or orange food coloring if desired, to enhance the color. Mix well.
6. Cook the mixture over medium heat, stirring frequently, until it thickens and starts to pull away from the sides of the pan. This usually takes about 15-20 minutes.
7. Continue to cook the mixture for another 5-10 minutes until it becomes very thick and glossy.
8. Immediately pour the hot mixture into the prepared baking dish. Smooth out the top with an oiled spatula or spoon.
9. Allow the Turkish delight to cool at room temperature for several hours, until it is completely set and firm.
10. Once set, lift the Turkish delight out of the baking dish using the parchment paper. Place it on a cutting board and cut it into small squares or rectangles using a sharp knife.
11. Dust the cut pieces with powdered sugar to prevent them from sticking together.
12. Your Mango Turkish Delight is now ready to be enjoyed! Store the pieces in an airtight container at room temperature for up to two weeks.

This Mango Turkish Delight recipe offers a refreshing tropical flavor and a chewy texture, making it a delightful treat for any occasion. Enjoy making and sharing this unique variation of Turkish delight with friends and family!

Pineapple Turkish Delight

Ingredients:

- 2 cups granulated sugar
- 1 cup water
- 1 tablespoon lemon juice
- 1 cup cornstarch
- 1 1/2 cups water
- 1 cup pineapple juice (freshly squeezed or canned)
- Yellow food coloring (optional)
- Powdered sugar, for dusting

Instructions:

1. Grease a square baking dish (about 8x8 inches) with oil and line it with parchment paper.
2. In a medium saucepan, combine the granulated sugar, 1 cup of water, and lemon juice. Stir over medium heat until the sugar dissolves completely.

3. In a separate bowl, mix the cornstarch with 1 1/2 cups of water until smooth and there are no lumps.
4. Gradually pour the cornstarch mixture into the saucepan with the sugar syrup, stirring constantly to prevent lumps.
5. Stir in the pineapple juice and add a few drops of yellow food coloring if desired, to enhance the color. Mix well.
6. Cook the mixture over medium heat, stirring frequently, until it thickens and starts to pull away from the sides of the pan. This usually takes about 15-20 minutes.
7. Continue to cook the mixture for another 5-10 minutes until it becomes very thick and glossy.
8. Immediately pour the hot mixture into the prepared baking dish. Smooth out the top with an oiled spatula or spoon.
9. Allow the Turkish delight to cool at room temperature for several hours, until it is completely set and firm.
10. Once set, lift the Turkish delight out of the baking dish using the parchment paper. Place it on a cutting board and cut it into small squares or rectangles using a sharp knife.
11. Dust the cut pieces with powdered sugar to prevent them from sticking together.
12. Your Pineapple Turkish Delight is now ready to be enjoyed! Store the pieces in an airtight container at room temperature for up to two weeks.

This Pineapple Turkish Delight recipe offers a tropical twist with the sweet and tangy flavor of pineapple, combined with the classic chewy texture of Turkish delight. It's a delightful treat for pineapple lovers and perfect for sharing on special occasions. Enjoy making and savoring this unique variation!

Cranberry Turkish Delight

Ingredients:

- 2 cups granulated sugar
- 1 cup water
- 1 tablespoon lemon juice
- 1 cup cornstarch
- 1 1/2 cups water
- 1 cup cranberry juice (freshly squeezed or store-bought)
- Red food coloring (optional)
- Powdered sugar, for dusting

Instructions:

1. Grease a square baking dish (about 8x8 inches) with oil and line it with parchment paper.
2. In a medium saucepan, combine the granulated sugar, 1 cup of water, and lemon juice. Stir over medium heat until the sugar dissolves completely.

3. In a separate bowl, mix the cornstarch with 1 1/2 cups of water until smooth and there are no lumps.
4. Gradually pour the cornstarch mixture into the saucepan with the sugar syrup, stirring constantly to prevent lumps.
5. Stir in the cranberry juice and add a few drops of red food coloring if desired, to enhance the color. Mix well.
6. Cook the mixture over medium heat, stirring frequently, until it thickens and starts to pull away from the sides of the pan. This usually takes about 15-20 minutes.
7. Continue to cook the mixture for another 5-10 minutes until it becomes very thick and glossy.
8. Immediately pour the hot mixture into the prepared baking dish. Smooth out the top with an oiled spatula or spoon.
9. Allow the Turkish delight to cool at room temperature for several hours, until it is completely set and firm.
10. Once set, lift the Turkish delight out of the baking dish using the parchment paper. Place it on a cutting board and cut it into small squares or rectangles using a sharp knife.
11. Dust the cut pieces with powdered sugar to prevent them from sticking together.
12. Your Cranberry Turkish Delight is now ready to be enjoyed! Store the pieces in an airtight container at room temperature for up to two weeks.

This Cranberry Turkish Delight recipe offers a delightful balance of tartness and sweetness, making it a unique and festive treat, especially around the holidays. Enjoy making and sharing this delicious confection with friends and family!

Ginger Turkish Delight

Ingredients:

- 2 cups granulated sugar
- 1 cup water
- 1 tablespoon lemon juice
- 1 cup cornstarch
- 1 1/2 cups water
- 2-3 tablespoons fresh ginger, finely grated
- Powdered sugar, for dusting

Instructions:

1. Grease a square baking dish (about 8x8 inches) with oil and line it with parchment paper.
2. In a medium saucepan, combine the granulated sugar, 1 cup of water, and lemon juice. Stir over medium heat until the sugar dissolves completely.
3. In a separate bowl, mix the cornstarch with 1 1/2 cups of water until smooth and there are no lumps.

4. Gradually pour the cornstarch mixture into the saucepan with the sugar syrup, stirring constantly to prevent lumps.
5. Stir in the finely grated fresh ginger. Adjust the amount to your taste preferences, keeping in mind that ginger has a strong flavor.
6. Cook the mixture over medium heat, stirring frequently, until it thickens and starts to pull away from the sides of the pan. This usually takes about 15-20 minutes.
7. Continue to cook the mixture for another 5-10 minutes until it becomes very thick and glossy.
8. Immediately pour the hot mixture into the prepared baking dish. Smooth out the top with an oiled spatula or spoon.
9. Allow the Turkish delight to cool at room temperature for several hours, until it is completely set and firm.
10. Once set, lift the Turkish delight out of the baking dish using the parchment paper. Place it on a cutting board and cut it into small squares or rectangles using a sharp knife.
11. Dust the cut pieces with powdered sugar to prevent them from sticking together.
12. Your Ginger Turkish Delight is now ready to be enjoyed! Store the pieces in an airtight container at room temperature for up to two weeks.

This Ginger Turkish Delight recipe offers a warming and spicy twist to the traditional treat, making it perfect for ginger enthusiasts. Enjoy making and savoring this unique variation of Turkish delight!

Cinnamon Turkish Delight

Ingredients:

- 2 cups granulated sugar
- 1 cup water
- 1 tablespoon lemon juice
- 1 cup cornstarch
- 1 1/2 cups water
- 2 teaspoons ground cinnamon
- Powdered sugar, for dusting

Instructions:

1. Grease a square baking dish (about 8x8 inches) with oil and line it with parchment paper.
2. In a medium saucepan, combine the granulated sugar, 1 cup of water, and lemon juice. Stir over medium heat until the sugar dissolves completely.
3. In a separate bowl, mix the cornstarch with 1 1/2 cups of water until smooth and there are no lumps.

4. Gradually pour the cornstarch mixture into the saucepan with the sugar syrup, stirring constantly to prevent lumps.
5. Stir in the ground cinnamon and mix well to incorporate.
6. Cook the mixture over medium heat, stirring frequently, until it thickens and starts to pull away from the sides of the pan. This usually takes about 15-20 minutes.
7. Continue to cook the mixture for another 5-10 minutes until it becomes very thick and glossy.
8. Immediately pour the hot mixture into the prepared baking dish. Smooth out the top with an oiled spatula or spoon.
9. Allow the Turkish delight to cool at room temperature for several hours, until it is completely set and firm.
10. Once set, lift the Turkish delight out of the baking dish using the parchment paper. Place it on a cutting board and cut it into small squares or rectangles using a sharp knife.
11. Dust the cut pieces with powdered sugar to prevent them from sticking together.
12. Your Cinnamon Turkish Delight is now ready to be enjoyed! Store the pieces in an airtight container at room temperature for up to two weeks.

This Cinnamon Turkish Delight recipe offers a cozy and aromatic variation of the classic treat, perfect for cinnamon lovers. Enjoy making and sharing this delightful confection!

Blueberry Turkish Delight

Ingredients:

- 2 cups granulated sugar
- 1 cup water
- 1 tablespoon lemon juice
- 1 cup cornstarch
- 1 1/2 cups water
- 1 cup blueberry puree (fresh or frozen)
- Blue food coloring (optional)
- Powdered sugar, for dusting

Instructions:

1. Grease a square baking dish (about 8x8 inches) with oil and line it with parchment paper.
2. In a medium saucepan, combine the granulated sugar, 1 cup of water, and lemon juice. Stir over medium heat until the sugar dissolves completely.
3. In a separate bowl, mix the cornstarch with 1 1/2 cups of water until smooth and there are no lumps.

4. Gradually pour the cornstarch mixture into the saucepan with the sugar syrup, stirring constantly to prevent lumps.
5. Stir in the blueberry puree and add a few drops of blue food coloring if desired, to enhance the color. Mix well.
6. Cook the mixture over medium heat, stirring frequently, until it thickens and starts to pull away from the sides of the pan. This usually takes about 15-20 minutes.
7. Continue to cook the mixture for another 5-10 minutes until it becomes very thick and glossy.
8. Immediately pour the hot mixture into the prepared baking dish. Smooth out the top with an oiled spatula or spoon.
9. Allow the Turkish delight to cool at room temperature for several hours, until it is completely set and firm.
10. Once set, lift the Turkish delight out of the baking dish using the parchment paper. Place it on a cutting board and cut it into small squares or rectangles using a sharp knife.
11. Dust the cut pieces with powdered sugar to prevent them from sticking together.
12. Your Blueberry Turkish Delight is now ready to be enjoyed! Store the pieces in an airtight container at room temperature for up to two weeks.

This Blueberry Turkish Delight recipe offers a refreshing and fruity twist to the traditional treat, perfect for those who enjoy the flavor of blueberries. Enjoy making and sharing this unique variation with friends and family!

Elderflower Turkish Delight

Ingredients:

- 2 cups granulated sugar
- 1 cup water
- 1 tablespoon lemon juice
- 1 cup cornstarch
- 1 1/2 cups water
- 1/2 cup elderflower cordial or elderflower syrup
- Powdered sugar, for dusting

Instructions:

1. Grease a square baking dish (about 8x8 inches) with oil and line it with parchment paper.
2. In a medium saucepan, combine the granulated sugar, 1 cup of water, and lemon juice. Stir over medium heat until the sugar dissolves completely.
3. In a separate bowl, mix the cornstarch with 1 1/2 cups of water until smooth and there are no lumps.
4. Gradually pour the cornstarch mixture into the saucepan with the sugar syrup, stirring constantly to prevent lumps.

5. Stir in the elderflower cordial or syrup. Mix well to incorporate the flavor throughout.
6. Cook the mixture over medium heat, stirring frequently, until it thickens and starts to pull away from the sides of the pan. This usually takes about 15-20 minutes.
7. Continue to cook the mixture for another 5-10 minutes until it becomes very thick and glossy.
8. Immediately pour the hot mixture into the prepared baking dish. Smooth out the top with an oiled spatula or spoon.
9. Allow the Turkish delight to cool at room temperature for several hours, until it is completely set and firm.
10. Once set, lift the Turkish delight out of the baking dish using the parchment paper. Place it on a cutting board and cut it into small squares or rectangles using a sharp knife.
11. Dust the cut pieces with powdered sugar to prevent them from sticking together.
12. Your Elderflower Turkish Delight is now ready to be enjoyed! Store the pieces in an airtight container at room temperature for up to two weeks.

This Elderflower Turkish Delight recipe offers a unique and floral twist to the traditional treat, perfect for those who appreciate delicate flavors. Enjoy making and sharing this delightful confection with friends and family!

Lavender Turkish Delight

Ingredients:

- 2 cups granulated sugar
- 1 cup water
- 1 tablespoon lemon juice
- 1 cup cornstarch
- 1 1/2 cups water
- 2 tablespoons culinary lavender buds (dried or fresh)
- Purple food coloring (optional)
- Powdered sugar, for dusting

Instructions:

1. Grease a square baking dish (about 8x8 inches) with oil and line it with parchment paper.
2. In a medium saucepan, combine the granulated sugar, 1 cup of water, and lemon juice. Stir over medium heat until the sugar dissolves completely.
3. In a separate bowl, mix the cornstarch with 1 1/2 cups of water until smooth and there are no lumps.
4. Crush the lavender buds slightly using a mortar and pestle to release their flavor. Add the crushed lavender buds to the sugar syrup mixture in the saucepan.

5. Gradually pour the cornstarch mixture into the saucepan with the sugar syrup and lavender, stirring constantly to prevent lumps.
6. If desired, add a few drops of purple food coloring to enhance the color. Mix well.
7. Cook the mixture over medium heat, stirring frequently, until it thickens and starts to pull away from the sides of the pan. This usually takes about 15-20 minutes.
8. Continue to cook the mixture for another 5-10 minutes until it becomes very thick and glossy.
9. Immediately pour the hot mixture into the prepared baking dish. Smooth out the top with an oiled spatula or spoon.
10. Allow the Turkish delight to cool at room temperature for several hours, until it is completely set and firm.
11. Once set, lift the Lavender Turkish delight out of the baking dish using the parchment paper. Place it on a cutting board and cut it into small squares or rectangles using a sharp knife.
12. Dust the cut pieces with powdered sugar to prevent them from sticking together.
13. Your Lavender Turkish Delight is now ready to be enjoyed! Store the pieces in an airtight container at room temperature for up to two weeks.

This Lavender Turkish Delight recipe offers a soothing and aromatic twist to the traditional treat, perfect for those who enjoy floral flavors. Enjoy making and sharing this delightful confection with friends and family!

Anise Turkish Delight

Ingredients:

- 2 cups granulated sugar
- 1 cup water
- 1 tablespoon lemon juice
- 1 cup cornstarch
- 1 1/2 cups water
- 1 tablespoon anise extract
- 1/2 teaspoon ground anise seeds (optional, for extra flavor)
- Powdered sugar, for dusting

Instructions:

1. Grease a square baking dish (about 8x8 inches) with oil and line it with parchment paper.
2. In a medium saucepan, combine the granulated sugar, 1 cup of water, and lemon juice. Stir over medium heat until the sugar dissolves completely.
3. In a separate bowl, mix the cornstarch with 1 1/2 cups of water until smooth and there are no lumps.
4. Gradually pour the cornstarch mixture into the saucepan with the sugar syrup, stirring constantly to prevent lumps.

5. Stir in the anise extract and ground anise seeds (if using). Mix well to distribute the flavor evenly.
6. Cook the mixture over medium heat, stirring frequently, until it thickens and starts to pull away from the sides of the pan. This usually takes about 15-20 minutes.
7. Continue to cook the mixture for another 5-10 minutes until it becomes very thick and glossy.
8. Immediately pour the hot mixture into the prepared baking dish. Smooth out the top with an oiled spatula or spoon.
9. Allow the Turkish delight to cool at room temperature for several hours, until it is completely set and firm.
10. Once set, lift the Turkish delight out of the baking dish using the parchment paper. Place it on a cutting board and cut it into small squares or rectangles using a sharp knife.
11. Dust the cut pieces with powdered sugar to prevent them from sticking together.
12. Your Anise Turkish Delight is now ready to be enjoyed! Store the pieces in an airtight container at room temperature for up to two weeks.

This Anise Turkish Delight recipe offers a distinctive licorice-like flavor that pairs well with the sweet and chewy texture of Turkish delight. Enjoy making and sharing this unique variation with friends and family!

Rosemary Turkish Delight

Ingredients:

- 2 cups granulated sugar
- 1 cup water
- 1 tablespoon lemon juice
- 1 cup cornstarch
- 1 1/2 cups water
- 2 tablespoons fresh rosemary leaves, finely chopped
- Powdered sugar, for dusting

Instructions:

1. Grease a square baking dish (about 8x8 inches) with oil and line it with parchment paper.
2. In a medium saucepan, combine the granulated sugar, 1 cup of water, and lemon juice. Stir over medium heat until the sugar dissolves completely.
3. In a separate bowl, mix the cornstarch with 1 1/2 cups of water until smooth and there are no lumps.
4. Add the finely chopped fresh rosemary leaves to the sugar syrup mixture in the saucepan.
5. Gradually pour the cornstarch mixture into the saucepan with the sugar syrup and rosemary, stirring constantly to prevent lumps.

6. Cook the mixture over medium heat, stirring frequently, until it thickens and starts to pull away from the sides of the pan. This usually takes about 15-20 minutes.
7. Continue to cook the mixture for another 5-10 minutes until it becomes very thick and glossy.
8. Immediately pour the hot mixture into the prepared baking dish. Smooth out the top with an oiled spatula or spoon.
9. Allow the Turkish delight to cool at room temperature for several hours, until it is completely set and firm.
10. Once set, lift the Rosemary Turkish delight out of the baking dish using the parchment paper. Place it on a cutting board and cut it into small squares or rectangles using a sharp knife.
11. Dust the cut pieces with powdered sugar to prevent them from sticking together.
12. Your Rosemary Turkish Delight is now ready to be enjoyed! Store the pieces in an airtight container at room temperature for up to two weeks.

This Rosemary Turkish Delight recipe offers a unique herbal flavor that complements the sweet and chewy texture of Turkish delight. Enjoy making and sharing this distinctive variation with friends and family!

Fig Turkish Delight

Ingredients:

- 1 cup dried figs, stemmed and chopped
- 2 cups granulated sugar
- 1 cup water
- 1 tablespoon lemon juice
- 1 cup cornstarch
- 1 1/2 cups water
- Powdered sugar, for dusting

Instructions:

1. Grease a square baking dish (about 8x8 inches) with oil and line it with parchment paper.
2. In a small saucepan, combine the chopped dried figs with enough water to cover them. Bring to a boil, then reduce heat and simmer for 10 minutes until the figs are soft and tender. Drain any excess water and set aside.
3. In a medium saucepan, combine the granulated sugar, 1 cup of water, and lemon juice. Stir over medium heat until the sugar dissolves completely.
4. In a separate bowl, mix the cornstarch with 1 1/2 cups of water until smooth and there are no lumps.
5. Gradually pour the cornstarch mixture into the saucepan with the sugar syrup, stirring constantly to prevent lumps.

6. Stir in the softened dried figs and mix well to incorporate.
7. Cook the mixture over medium heat, stirring frequently, until it thickens and starts to pull away from the sides of the pan. This usually takes about 15-20 minutes.
8. Continue to cook the mixture for another 5-10 minutes until it becomes very thick and glossy.
9. Immediately pour the hot mixture into the prepared baking dish. Smooth out the top with an oiled spatula or spoon.
10. Allow the Turkish delight to cool at room temperature for several hours, until it is completely set and firm.
11. Once set, lift the Fig Turkish delight out of the baking dish using the parchment paper. Place it on a cutting board and cut it into small squares or rectangles using a sharp knife.
12. Dust the cut pieces with powdered sugar to prevent them from sticking together.
13. Your Fig Turkish Delight is now ready to be enjoyed! Store the pieces in an airtight container at room temperature for up to two weeks.

This Fig Turkish Delight recipe offers a deliciously fruity and chewy variation of the traditional treat, perfect for fig lovers. Enjoy making and sharing this unique confection with friends and family!

Date Turkish Delight

Ingredients:

- 1 cup pitted dates, chopped
- 2 cups granulated sugar
- 1 cup water
- 1 tablespoon lemon juice
- 1 cup cornstarch
- 1 1/2 cups water
- Powdered sugar, for dusting

Instructions:

1. Grease a square baking dish (about 8x8 inches) with oil and line it with parchment paper.
2. In a small saucepan, combine the chopped dates with enough water to cover them. Bring to a boil, then reduce heat and simmer for 10 minutes until the dates are soft and tender. Drain any excess water and set aside.
3. In a medium saucepan, combine the granulated sugar, 1 cup of water, and lemon juice. Stir over medium heat until the sugar dissolves completely.
4. In a separate bowl, mix the cornstarch with 1 1/2 cups of water until smooth and there are no lumps.
5. Gradually pour the cornstarch mixture into the saucepan with the sugar syrup, stirring constantly to prevent lumps.
6. Stir in the softened chopped dates and mix well to incorporate.

7. Cook the mixture over medium heat, stirring frequently, until it thickens and starts to pull away from the sides of the pan. This usually takes about 15-20 minutes.
8. Continue to cook the mixture for another 5-10 minutes until it becomes very thick and glossy.
9. Immediately pour the hot mixture into the prepared baking dish. Smooth out the top with an oiled spatula or spoon.
10. Allow the Turkish delight to cool at room temperature for several hours, until it is completely set and firm.
11. Once set, lift the Date Turkish delight out of the baking dish using the parchment paper. Place it on a cutting board and cut it into small squares or rectangles using a sharp knife.
12. Dust the cut pieces with powdered sugar to prevent them from sticking together.
13. Your Date Turkish Delight is now ready to be enjoyed! Store the pieces in an airtight container at room temperature for up to two weeks.

This Date Turkish Delight recipe offers a naturally sweet and chewy variation of the traditional treat, perfect for date enthusiasts. Enjoy making and sharing this unique confection with friends and family!

Mulberry Turkish Delight

Ingredients:

- 1 cup fresh mulberries, washed and stems removed (or substitute with frozen mulberries)
- 2 cups granulated sugar
- 1 cup water
- 1 tablespoon lemon juice
- 1 cup cornstarch
- 1 1/2 cups water
- Powdered sugar, for dusting

Instructions:

1. Grease a square baking dish (about 8x8 inches) with oil and line it with parchment paper.
2. In a small saucepan, combine the fresh mulberries with enough water to cover them. Bring to a boil, then reduce heat and simmer for 10 minutes until the mulberries are soft and tender. If using frozen mulberries, simply thaw them.
3. Mash the mulberries with a fork or blend them briefly to create a puree. Strain the mixture through a fine-mesh sieve to remove seeds, if desired. Set aside the mulberry puree.
4. In a medium saucepan, combine the granulated sugar, 1 cup of water, and lemon juice. Stir over medium heat until the sugar dissolves completely.
5. In a separate bowl, mix the cornstarch with 1 1/2 cups of water until smooth and there are no lumps.

6. Gradually pour the cornstarch mixture into the saucepan with the sugar syrup, stirring constantly to prevent lumps.
7. Stir in the mulberry puree and mix well to incorporate the flavor throughout.
8. Cook the mixture over medium heat, stirring frequently, until it thickens and starts to pull away from the sides of the pan. This usually takes about 15-20 minutes.
9. Continue to cook the mixture for another 5-10 minutes until it becomes very thick and glossy.
10. Immediately pour the hot mixture into the prepared baking dish. Smooth out the top with an oiled spatula or spoon.
11. Allow the Turkish delight to cool at room temperature for several hours, until it is completely set and firm.
12. Once set, lift the Mulberry Turkish delight out of the baking dish using the parchment paper. Place it on a cutting board and cut it into small squares or rectangles using a sharp knife.
13. Dust the cut pieces with powdered sugar to prevent them from sticking together.
14. Your Mulberry Turkish Delight is now ready to be enjoyed! Store the pieces in an airtight container at room temperature for up to two weeks.

This Mulberry Turkish Delight recipe offers a delightful and fruity twist to the traditional treat, perfect for mulberry enthusiasts. Enjoy making and sharing this unique confection with friends and family!

Tamarind Turkish Delight

Ingredients:

- 1 cup tamarind paste
- 2 cups granulated sugar
- 1 cup water
- 1 tablespoon lemon juice
- 1 cup cornstarch
- 1 1/2 cups water
- Powdered sugar, for dusting

Instructions:

1. Grease a square baking dish (about 8x8 inches) with oil and line it with parchment paper.
2. In a small bowl, mix the tamarind paste with enough warm water to create a smooth consistency. Set aside.
3. In a medium saucepan, combine the granulated sugar, 1 cup of water, and lemon juice. Stir over medium heat until the sugar dissolves completely.
4. In a separate bowl, mix the cornstarch with 1 1/2 cups of water until smooth and there are no lumps.
5. Gradually pour the cornstarch mixture into the saucepan with the sugar syrup, stirring constantly to prevent lumps.
6. Stir in the tamarind paste mixture and mix well to incorporate the flavor throughout.
7. Cook the mixture over medium heat, stirring frequently, until it thickens and starts to pull away from the sides of the pan. This usually takes about 15-20 minutes.
8. Continue to cook the mixture for another 5-10 minutes until it becomes very thick and glossy.

9. Immediately pour the hot mixture into the prepared baking dish. Smooth out the top with an oiled spatula or spoon.
10. Allow the Turkish delight to cool at room temperature for several hours, until it is completely set and firm.
11. Once set, lift the Tamarind Turkish delight out of the baking dish using the parchment paper. Place it on a cutting board and cut it into small squares or rectangles using a sharp knife.
12. Dust the cut pieces with powdered sugar to prevent them from sticking together.
13. Your Tamarind Turkish Delight is now ready to be enjoyed! Store the pieces in an airtight container at room temperature for up to two weeks.

This Tamarind Turkish Delight recipe offers a tangy and exotic twist to the traditional treat, perfect for those who enjoy unique flavors. Enjoy making and sharing this delightful confection with friends and family!

Grape Turkish Delight

Ingredients:

- 1 cup grape juice (preferably freshly squeezed or 100% pure grape juice)
- 2 cups granulated sugar
- 1 cup water
- 1 tablespoon lemon juice
- 1 cup cornstarch
- 1 1/2 cups water
- Powdered sugar, for dusting

Instructions:

1. Grease a square baking dish (about 8x8 inches) with oil and line it with parchment paper.
2. In a medium saucepan, combine the grape juice, granulated sugar, 1 cup of water, and lemon juice. Stir over medium heat until the sugar dissolves completely.
3. In a separate bowl, mix the cornstarch with 1 1/2 cups of water until smooth and there are no lumps.
4. Gradually pour the cornstarch mixture into the saucepan with the grape juice mixture, stirring constantly to prevent lumps.
5. Cook the mixture over medium heat, stirring frequently, until it thickens and starts to pull away from the sides of the pan. This usually takes about 15-20 minutes.
6. Continue to cook the mixture for another 5-10 minutes until it becomes very thick and glossy.
7. Immediately pour the hot mixture into the prepared baking dish. Smooth out the top with an oiled spatula or spoon.
8. Allow the Turkish delight to cool at room temperature for several hours, until it is completely set and firm.

9. Once set, lift the Grape Turkish delight out of the baking dish using the parchment paper. Place it on a cutting board and cut it into small squares or rectangles using a sharp knife.
10. Dust the cut pieces with powdered sugar to prevent them from sticking together.
11. Your Grape Turkish Delight is now ready to be enjoyed! Store the pieces in an airtight container at room temperature for up to two weeks.

This Grape Turkish Delight recipe offers a refreshing and fruity twist to the traditional treat, perfect for grape enthusiasts. Enjoy making and sharing this delightful confection with friends and family!

Plum Turkish Delight

Ingredients:

- 1 cup fresh plums, pitted and chopped
- 2 cups granulated sugar
- 1 cup water
- 1 tablespoon lemon juice
- 1 cup cornstarch
- 1 1/2 cups water
- Powdered sugar, for dusting

Instructions:

1. Grease a square baking dish (about 8x8 inches) with oil and line it with parchment paper.
2. In a small saucepan, combine the chopped fresh plums with enough water to cover them. Bring to a boil, then reduce heat and simmer for 10 minutes until the plums are soft and tender.
3. Mash the cooked plums with a fork or blend them briefly to create a puree. Strain the mixture through a fine-mesh sieve to remove skins and seeds, if desired. Set aside the plum puree.
4. In a medium saucepan, combine the granulated sugar, 1 cup of water, and lemon juice. Stir over medium heat until the sugar dissolves completely.
5. In a separate bowl, mix the cornstarch with 1 1/2 cups of water until smooth and there are no lumps.
6. Gradually pour the cornstarch mixture into the saucepan with the sugar syrup, stirring constantly to prevent lumps.
7. Stir in the plum puree and mix well to incorporate the flavor throughout.
8. Cook the mixture over medium heat, stirring frequently, until it thickens and starts to pull away from the sides of the pan. This usually takes about 15-20 minutes.

9. Continue to cook the mixture for another 5-10 minutes until it becomes very thick and glossy.
10. Immediately pour the hot mixture into the prepared baking dish. Smooth out the top with an oiled spatula or spoon.
11. Allow the Turkish delight to cool at room temperature for several hours, until it is completely set and firm.
12. Once set, lift the Plum Turkish delight out of the baking dish using the parchment paper. Place it on a cutting board and cut it into small squares or rectangles using a sharp knife.
13. Dust the cut pieces with powdered sugar to prevent them from sticking together.
14. Your Plum Turkish Delight is now ready to be enjoyed! Store the pieces in an airtight container at room temperature for up to two weeks.

This Plum Turkish Delight recipe offers a sweet and tangy twist to the traditional treat, perfect for plum enthusiasts. Enjoy making and sharing this delightful confection with friends and family!

Lychee Turkish Delight

Ingredients:

- 1 cup lychee puree (from canned or fresh lychees)
- 2 cups granulated sugar
- 1 cup water
- 1 tablespoon lemon juice
- 1 cup cornstarch
- 1 1/2 cups water
- Powdered sugar, for dusting

Instructions:

1. Grease a square baking dish (about 8x8 inches) with oil and line it with parchment paper.
2. If using canned lychees, drain them and remove any seeds. If using fresh lychees, peel and pit them, then blend or process into a smooth puree. Measure out 1 cup of lychee puree.
3. In a medium saucepan, combine the granulated sugar, 1 cup of water, and lemon juice. Stir over medium heat until the sugar dissolves completely.
4. In a separate bowl, mix the cornstarch with 1 1/2 cups of water until smooth and there are no lumps.
5. Gradually pour the cornstarch mixture into the saucepan with the sugar syrup, stirring constantly to prevent lumps.
6. Stir in the lychee puree and mix well to incorporate the flavor throughout.
7. Cook the mixture over medium heat, stirring frequently, until it thickens and starts to pull away from the sides of the pan. This usually takes about 15-20 minutes.
8. Continue to cook the mixture for another 5-10 minutes until it becomes very thick and glossy.

9. Immediately pour the hot mixture into the prepared baking dish. Smooth out the top with an oiled spatula or spoon.
10. Allow the Turkish delight to cool at room temperature for several hours, until it is completely set and firm.
11. Once set, lift the Lychee Turkish delight out of the baking dish using the parchment paper. Place it on a cutting board and cut it into small squares or rectangles using a sharp knife.
12. Dust the cut pieces with powdered sugar to prevent them from sticking together.
13. Your Lychee Turkish Delight is now ready to be enjoyed! Store the pieces in an airtight container at room temperature for up to two weeks.

This Lychee Turkish Delight recipe offers a delightful and exotic twist to the traditional treat, perfect for lychee enthusiasts. Enjoy making and sharing this unique confection with friends and family!

Passionfruit Turkish Delight

Ingredients:

- 1 cup passionfruit pulp (strained to remove seeds)
- 2 cups granulated sugar
- 1 cup water
- 1 tablespoon lemon juice
- 1 cup cornstarch
- 1 1/2 cups water
- Powdered sugar, for dusting

Instructions:

1. Grease a square baking dish (about 8x8 inches) with oil and line it with parchment paper.
2. Strain the passionfruit pulp to remove seeds and measure out 1 cup of strained pulp.
3. In a medium saucepan, combine the granulated sugar, 1 cup of water, and lemon juice. Stir over medium heat until the sugar dissolves completely.
4. In a separate bowl, mix the cornstarch with 1 1/2 cups of water until smooth and there are no lumps.
5. Gradually pour the cornstarch mixture into the saucepan with the sugar syrup, stirring constantly to prevent lumps.
6. Stir in the passionfruit pulp and mix well to incorporate the flavor throughout.
7. Cook the mixture over medium heat, stirring frequently, until it thickens and starts to pull away from the sides of the pan. This usually takes about 15-20 minutes.
8. Continue to cook the mixture for another 5-10 minutes until it becomes very thick and glossy.
9. Immediately pour the hot mixture into the prepared baking dish. Smooth out the top with an oiled spatula or spoon.

10. Allow the Turkish delight to cool at room temperature for several hours, until it is completely set and firm.
11. Once set, lift the Passionfruit Turkish delight out of the baking dish using the parchment paper. Place it on a cutting board and cut it into small squares or rectangles using a sharp knife.
12. Dust the cut pieces with powdered sugar to prevent them from sticking together.
13. Your Passionfruit Turkish Delight is now ready to be enjoyed! Store the pieces in an airtight container at room temperature for up to two weeks.

This Passionfruit Turkish Delight recipe offers a tropical and tangy variation of the traditional treat, perfect for passionfruit lovers. Enjoy making and sharing this delightful confection with friends and family!

Kiwi Turkish Delight

Ingredients:

- 1 cup kiwi puree (from ripe kiwis)
- 2 cups granulated sugar
- 1 cup water
- 1 tablespoon lemon juice
- 1 cup cornstarch
- 1 1/2 cups water
- Powdered sugar, for dusting

Instructions:

1. Grease a square baking dish (about 8x8 inches) with oil and line it with parchment paper.
2. Peel ripe kiwis and blend them until smooth to create 1 cup of kiwi puree.
3. In a medium saucepan, combine the granulated sugar, 1 cup of water, and lemon juice. Stir over medium heat until the sugar dissolves completely.
4. In a separate bowl, mix the cornstarch with 1 1/2 cups of water until smooth and there are no lumps.
5. Gradually pour the cornstarch mixture into the saucepan with the sugar syrup, stirring constantly to prevent lumps.
6. Stir in the kiwi puree and mix well to incorporate the flavor throughout.
7. Cook the mixture over medium heat, stirring frequently, until it thickens and starts to pull away from the sides of the pan. This usually takes about 15-20 minutes.
8. Continue to cook the mixture for another 5-10 minutes until it becomes very thick and glossy.
9. Immediately pour the hot mixture into the prepared baking dish. Smooth out the top with an oiled spatula or spoon.

10. Allow the Turkish delight to cool at room temperature for several hours, until it is completely set and firm.
11. Once set, lift the Kiwi Turkish delight out of the baking dish using the parchment paper. Place it on a cutting board and cut it into small squares or rectangles using a sharp knife.
12. Dust the cut pieces with powdered sugar to prevent them from sticking together.
13. Your Kiwi Turkish Delight is now ready to be enjoyed! Store the pieces in an airtight container at room temperature for up to two weeks.

This Kiwi Turkish Delight recipe offers a fresh and vibrant flavor to the traditional treat, perfect for kiwi enthusiasts. Enjoy making and sharing this delightful confection with friends and family!

Guava Turkish Delight

Ingredients:

- 1 cup guava pulp (strained to remove seeds)
- 2 cups granulated sugar
- 1 cup water
- 1 tablespoon lemon juice
- 1 cup cornstarch
- 1 1/2 cups water
- Powdered sugar, for dusting

Instructions:

1. Grease a square baking dish (about 8x8 inches) with oil and line it with parchment paper.
2. Strain the guava pulp to remove seeds and measure out 1 cup of strained pulp.
3. In a medium saucepan, combine the granulated sugar, 1 cup of water, and lemon juice. Stir over medium heat until the sugar dissolves completely.
4. In a separate bowl, mix the cornstarch with 1 1/2 cups of water until smooth and there are no lumps.
5. Gradually pour the cornstarch mixture into the saucepan with the sugar syrup, stirring constantly to prevent lumps.
6. Stir in the guava pulp and mix well to incorporate the flavor throughout.
7. Cook the mixture over medium heat, stirring frequently, until it thickens and starts to pull away from the sides of the pan. This usually takes about 15-20 minutes.
8. Continue to cook the mixture for another 5-10 minutes until it becomes very thick and glossy.
9. Immediately pour the hot mixture into the prepared baking dish. Smooth out the top with an oiled spatula or spoon.

10. Allow the Turkish delight to cool at room temperature for several hours, until it is completely set and firm.
11. Once set, lift the Guava Turkish delight out of the baking dish using the parchment paper. Place it on a cutting board and cut it into small squares or rectangles using a sharp knife.
12. Dust the cut pieces with powdered sugar to prevent them from sticking together.
13. Your Guava Turkish Delight is now ready to be enjoyed! Store the pieces in an airtight container at room temperature for up to two weeks.

This Guava Turkish Delight recipe offers a tropical and exotic twist to the traditional treat, perfect for guava enthusiasts. Enjoy making and sharing this delightful confection with friends and family!

Watermelon Turkish Delight

Ingredients:

- 1 cup watermelon juice (strained to remove pulp)
- 2 cups granulated sugar
- 1 cup water
- 1 tablespoon lemon juice
- 1 cup cornstarch
- 1 1/2 cups water
- Powdered sugar, for dusting

Instructions:

1. Grease a square baking dish (about 8x8 inches) with oil and line it with parchment paper.
2. Strain the watermelon juice to remove any pulp and measure out 1 cup of strained juice.
3. In a medium saucepan, combine the granulated sugar, 1 cup of water, and lemon juice. Stir over medium heat until the sugar dissolves completely.
4. In a separate bowl, mix the cornstarch with 1 1/2 cups of water until smooth and there are no lumps.
5. Gradually pour the cornstarch mixture into the saucepan with the sugar syrup, stirring constantly to prevent lumps.
6. Stir in the watermelon juice and mix well to incorporate the flavor throughout.
7. Cook the mixture over medium heat, stirring frequently, until it thickens and starts to pull away from the sides of the pan. This usually takes about 15-20 minutes.
8. Continue to cook the mixture for another 5-10 minutes until it becomes very thick and glossy.
9. Immediately pour the hot mixture into the prepared baking dish. Smooth out the top with an oiled spatula or spoon.

10. Allow the Turkish delight to cool at room temperature for several hours, until it is completely set and firm.
11. Once set, lift the Watermelon Turkish delight out of the baking dish using the parchment paper. Place it on a cutting board and cut it into small squares or rectangles using a sharp knife.
12. Dust the cut pieces with powdered sugar to prevent them from sticking together.
13. Your Watermelon Turkish Delight is now ready to be enjoyed! Store the pieces in an airtight container at room temperature for up to two weeks.

This Watermelon Turkish Delight recipe offers a delightful and refreshing twist to the traditional treat, perfect for watermelon lovers. Enjoy making and sharing this unique confection with friends and family!

Papaya Turkish Delight

Ingredients:

- 1 cup papaya puree (from ripe papaya)
- 2 cups granulated sugar
- 1 cup water
- 1 tablespoon lemon juice
- 1 cup cornstarch
- 1 1/2 cups water
- Powdered sugar, for dusting

Instructions:

1. Grease a square baking dish (about 8x8 inches) with oil and line it with parchment paper.
2. Peel and remove the seeds from a ripe papaya. Cut the papaya into chunks and blend or process until smooth to create 1 cup of papaya puree.
3. In a medium saucepan, combine the granulated sugar, 1 cup of water, and lemon juice. Stir over medium heat until the sugar dissolves completely.
4. In a separate bowl, mix the cornstarch with 1 1/2 cups of water until smooth and there are no lumps.
5. Gradually pour the cornstarch mixture into the saucepan with the sugar syrup, stirring constantly to prevent lumps.
6. Stir in the papaya puree and mix well to incorporate the flavor throughout.
7. Cook the mixture over medium heat, stirring frequently, until it thickens and starts to pull away from the sides of the pan. This usually takes about 15-20 minutes.
8. Continue to cook the mixture for another 5-10 minutes until it becomes very thick and glossy.
9. Immediately pour the hot mixture into the prepared baking dish. Smooth out the top with an oiled spatula or spoon.

10. Allow the Turkish delight to cool at room temperature for several hours, until it is completely set and firm.
11. Once set, lift the Papaya Turkish delight out of the baking dish using the parchment paper. Place it on a cutting board and cut it into small squares or rectangles using a sharp knife.
12. Dust the cut pieces with powdered sugar to prevent them from sticking together.
13. Your Papaya Turkish Delight is now ready to be enjoyed! Store the pieces in an airtight container at room temperature for up to two weeks.

This Papaya Turkish Delight recipe offers a tropical and fruity twist to the traditional treat, perfect for papaya enthusiasts. Enjoy making and sharing this delightful confection with friends and family!

Pear Turkish Delight

Ingredients:

- 1 cup pear puree (from ripe pears)
- 2 cups granulated sugar
- 1 cup water
- 1 tablespoon lemon juice
- 1 cup cornstarch
- 1 1/2 cups water
- Powdered sugar, for dusting

Instructions:

1. Grease a square baking dish (about 8x8 inches) with oil and line it with parchment paper.
2. Peel and core ripe pears. Cut them into chunks and blend or process until smooth to create 1 cup of pear puree.
3. In a medium saucepan, combine the granulated sugar, 1 cup of water, and lemon juice. Stir over medium heat until the sugar dissolves completely.
4. In a separate bowl, mix the cornstarch with 1 1/2 cups of water until smooth and there are no lumps.
5. Gradually pour the cornstarch mixture into the saucepan with the sugar syrup, stirring constantly to prevent lumps.
6. Stir in the pear puree and mix well to incorporate the flavor throughout.
7. Cook the mixture over medium heat, stirring frequently, until it thickens and starts to pull away from the sides of the pan. This usually takes about 15-20 minutes.
8. Continue to cook the mixture for another 5-10 minutes until it becomes very thick and glossy.
9. Immediately pour the hot mixture into the prepared baking dish. Smooth out the top with an oiled spatula or spoon.

10. Allow the Turkish delight to cool at room temperature for several hours, until it is completely set and firm.
11. Once set, lift the Pear Turkish delight out of the baking dish using the parchment paper. Place it on a cutting board and cut it into small squares or rectangles using a sharp knife.
12. Dust the cut pieces with powdered sugar to prevent them from sticking together.
13. Your Pear Turkish Delight is now ready to be enjoyed! Store the pieces in an airtight container at room temperature for up to two weeks.

This Pear Turkish Delight recipe offers a sweet and subtle flavor, perfect for pear enthusiasts. Enjoy making and sharing this delightful confection with friends and family!

Quince Turkish Delight

Ingredients:

- 2 cups quince puree (from ripe quinces)
- 2 cups granulated sugar
- 1 cup water
- 1 tablespoon lemon juice
- 1 cup cornstarch
- 1 1/2 cups water
- Powdered sugar, for dusting

Instructions:

1. Grease a square baking dish (about 8x8 inches) with oil and line it with parchment paper.
2. Peel and core ripe quinces. Cut them into chunks and cook them in water until tender. Blend or process until smooth to create 2 cups of quince puree.
3. In a medium saucepan, combine the granulated sugar, 1 cup of water, and lemon juice. Stir over medium heat until the sugar dissolves completely.
4. In a separate bowl, mix the cornstarch with 1 1/2 cups of water until smooth and there are no lumps.
5. Gradually pour the cornstarch mixture into the saucepan with the sugar syrup, stirring constantly to prevent lumps.
6. Stir in the quince puree and mix well to incorporate the flavor throughout.
7. Cook the mixture over medium heat, stirring frequently, until it thickens and starts to pull away from the sides of the pan. This usually takes about 15-20 minutes.
8. Continue to cook the mixture for another 5-10 minutes until it becomes very thick and glossy.
9. Immediately pour the hot mixture into the prepared baking dish. Smooth out the top with an oiled spatula or spoon.

10. Allow the Turkish delight to cool at room temperature for several hours, until it is completely set and firm.
11. Once set, lift the Quince Turkish delight out of the baking dish using the parchment paper. Place it on a cutting board and cut it into small squares or rectangles using a sharp knife.
12. Dust the cut pieces with powdered sugar to prevent them from sticking together.
13. Your Quince Turkish Delight is now ready to be enjoyed! Store the pieces in an airtight container at room temperature for up to two weeks.

This Quince Turkish Delight recipe offers a fragrant and subtly sweet flavor, perfect for quince enthusiasts. Enjoy making and sharing this delightful confection with friends and family!

Nectarine Turkish Delight

Ingredients:

- 2 cups nectarine puree (from ripe nectarines)
- 2 cups granulated sugar
- 1 cup water
- 1 tablespoon lemon juice
- 1 cup cornstarch
- 1 1/2 cups water
- Powdered sugar, for dusting

Instructions:

1. Grease a square baking dish (about 8x8 inches) with oil and line it with parchment paper.
2. Peel and pit ripe nectarines. Cut them into chunks and blend or process until smooth to create 2 cups of nectarine puree.
3. In a medium saucepan, combine the granulated sugar, 1 cup of water, and lemon juice. Stir over medium heat until the sugar dissolves completely.
4. In a separate bowl, mix the cornstarch with 1 1/2 cups of water until smooth and there are no lumps.
5. Gradually pour the cornstarch mixture into the saucepan with the sugar syrup, stirring constantly to prevent lumps.
6. Stir in the nectarine puree and mix well to incorporate the flavor throughout.
7. Cook the mixture over medium heat, stirring frequently, until it thickens and starts to pull away from the sides of the pan. This usually takes about 15-20 minutes.
8. Continue to cook the mixture for another 5-10 minutes until it becomes very thick and glossy.
9. Immediately pour the hot mixture into the prepared baking dish. Smooth out the top with an oiled spatula or spoon.

10. Allow the Turkish delight to cool at room temperature for several hours, until it is completely set and firm.
11. Once set, lift the Nectarine Turkish delight out of the baking dish using the parchment paper. Place it on a cutting board and cut it into small squares or rectangles using a sharp knife.
12. Dust the cut pieces with powdered sugar to prevent them from sticking together.
13. Your Nectarine Turkish Delight is now ready to be enjoyed! Store the pieces in an airtight container at room temperature for up to two weeks.

This Nectarine Turkish Delight recipe offers a sweet and fruity flavor, perfect for nectarine enthusiasts. Enjoy making and sharing this delightful confection with friends and family!

Persimmon Turkish Delight

Ingredients:

- 2 cups persimmon puree (from ripe persimmons)
- 2 cups granulated sugar
- 1 cup water
- 1 tablespoon lemon juice
- 1 cup cornstarch
- 1 1/2 cups water
- Powdered sugar, for dusting

Instructions:

1. Grease a square baking dish (about 8x8 inches) with oil and line it with parchment paper.
2. Peel ripe persimmons and remove any seeds. Cut them into chunks and blend or process until smooth to create 2 cups of persimmon puree.
3. In a medium saucepan, combine the granulated sugar, 1 cup of water, and lemon juice. Stir over medium heat until the sugar dissolves completely.
4. In a separate bowl, mix the cornstarch with 1 1/2 cups of water until smooth and there are no lumps.
5. Gradually pour the cornstarch mixture into the saucepan with the sugar syrup, stirring constantly to prevent lumps.
6. Stir in the persimmon puree and mix well to incorporate the flavor throughout.
7. Cook the mixture over medium heat, stirring frequently, until it thickens and starts to pull away from the sides of the pan. This usually takes about 15-20 minutes.
8. Continue to cook the mixture for another 5-10 minutes until it becomes very thick and glossy.
9. Immediately pour the hot mixture into the prepared baking dish. Smooth out the top with an oiled spatula or spoon.

10. Allow the Turkish delight to cool at room temperature for several hours, until it is completely set and firm.
11. Once set, lift the Persimmon Turkish delight out of the baking dish using the parchment paper. Place it on a cutting board and cut it into small squares or rectangles using a sharp knife.
12. Dust the cut pieces with powdered sugar to prevent them from sticking together.
13. Your Persimmon Turkish Delight is now ready to be enjoyed! Store the pieces in an airtight container at room temperature for up to two weeks.

This Persimmon Turkish Delight recipe offers a sweet and fruity flavor with a hint of tanginess, perfect for persimmon enthusiasts. Enjoy making and sharing this delightful confection with friends and family!

Caramel Turkish Delight

Ingredients:

- 2 cups granulated sugar
- 1 cup water
- 1 tablespoon lemon juice
- 1 cup cornstarch
- 1 1/2 cups water
- 1/2 cup unsalted butter
- 1 cup sweetened condensed milk
- Powdered sugar, for dusting

Instructions:

1. Grease a square baking dish (about 8x8 inches) with butter or oil and line it with parchment paper.
2. In a medium saucepan, combine the granulated sugar, 1 cup of water, and lemon juice. Stir over medium heat until the sugar dissolves completely.
3. In a separate bowl, mix the cornstarch with 1 1/2 cups of water until smooth and there are no lumps.
4. Gradually pour the cornstarch mixture into the saucepan with the sugar syrup, stirring constantly to prevent lumps.
5. Add the unsalted butter to the mixture and continue stirring until the butter is melted and fully incorporated.
6. Stir in the sweetened condensed milk and mix well.
7. Cook the mixture over medium heat, stirring frequently, until it thickens and starts to pull away from the sides of the pan. This usually takes about 15-20 minutes.
8. Continue to cook the mixture for another 5-10 minutes until it becomes very thick and glossy, resembling caramel.

9. Immediately pour the hot caramel mixture into the prepared baking dish. Smooth out the top with an oiled spatula or spoon.
10. Allow the Turkish delight to cool at room temperature for several hours, until it is completely set and firm.
11. Once set, lift the Caramel Turkish delight out of the baking dish using the parchment paper. Place it on a cutting board and cut it into small squares or rectangles using a sharp knife.
12. Dust the cut pieces with powdered sugar to prevent them from sticking together.
13. Your Caramel Turkish Delight is now ready to be enjoyed! Store the pieces in an airtight container at room temperature for up to two weeks.

This Caramel Turkish Delight recipe offers a decadent and creamy flavor, perfect for caramel lovers. Enjoy making and sharing this luxurious confection with friends and family!

Pistachio-Rose Turkish Delight

Ingredients:

- 1 cup shelled pistachios, finely chopped
- 2 cups granulated sugar
- 1 cup water
- 1 tablespoon lemon juice
- 1/2 cup cornstarch
- 1 1/2 cups water
- 2 tablespoons rose water
- Pink food coloring (optional)
- Powdered sugar, for dusting

Instructions:

1. Grease a square baking dish (about 8x8 inches) with oil and line it with parchment paper.
2. In a medium saucepan, combine the granulated sugar, 1 cup of water, and lemon juice. Stir over medium heat until the sugar dissolves completely.
3. In a separate bowl, mix the cornstarch with 1 1/2 cups of water until smooth and there are no lumps.
4. Gradually pour the cornstarch mixture into the saucepan with the sugar syrup, stirring constantly to prevent lumps.
5. Cook the mixture over medium heat, stirring frequently, until it thickens and starts to pull away from the sides of the pan. This usually takes about 15-20 minutes.
6. Stir in the finely chopped pistachios and continue to cook for another 5-10 minutes until the mixture becomes very thick and glossy.
7. Add the rose water and mix well. If desired, add a few drops of pink food coloring to achieve a light pink color (optional).

8. Immediately pour the hot mixture into the prepared baking dish. Smooth out the top with an oiled spatula or spoon.
9. Allow the Turkish delight to cool at room temperature for several hours, until it is completely set and firm.
10. Once set, lift the Pistachio-Rose Turkish delight out of the baking dish using the parchment paper. Place it on a cutting board and cut it into small squares or rectangles using a sharp knife.
11. Dust the cut pieces with powdered sugar to prevent them from sticking together.
12. Your Pistachio-Rose Turkish Delight is now ready to be enjoyed! Store the pieces in an airtight container at room temperature for up to two weeks.

This Pistachio-Rose Turkish Delight recipe offers a perfect blend of floral and nutty flavors, making it a delightful treat for special occasions or as a homemade gift. Enjoy making and sharing this exquisite confection with friends and family!

Orange Blossom Turkish Delight

Ingredients:

- 2 cups granulated sugar
- 1 cup water
- 1 tablespoon lemon juice
- Zest of 1 orange (optional, for added flavor)
- 1/2 cup cornstarch
- 1 1/2 cups water
- 2 tablespoons orange blossom water
- Orange food coloring (optional)
- Powdered sugar, for dusting

Instructions:

1. Grease a square baking dish (about 8x8 inches) with oil and line it with parchment paper.
2. In a medium saucepan, combine the granulated sugar, 1 cup of water, lemon juice, and orange zest (if using). Stir over medium heat until the sugar dissolves completely.
3. In a separate bowl, mix the cornstarch with 1 1/2 cups of water until smooth and there are no lumps.
4. Gradually pour the cornstarch mixture into the saucepan with the sugar syrup, stirring constantly to prevent lumps.
5. Cook the mixture over medium heat, stirring frequently, until it thickens and starts to pull away from the sides of the pan. This usually takes about 15-20 minutes.
6. Stir in the orange blossom water and mix well. If desired, add a few drops of orange food coloring to achieve a light orange color (optional).
7. Continue to cook the mixture for another 5-10 minutes until it becomes very thick and glossy.

8. Immediately pour the hot mixture into the prepared baking dish. Smooth out the top with an oiled spatula or spoon.
9. Allow the Turkish delight to cool at room temperature for several hours, until it is completely set and firm.
10. Once set, lift the Orange Blossom Turkish delight out of the baking dish using the parchment paper. Place it on a cutting board and cut it into small squares or rectangles using a sharp knife.
11. Dust the cut pieces with powdered sugar to prevent them from sticking together.
12. Your Orange Blossom Turkish Delight is now ready to be enjoyed! Store the pieces in an airtight container at room temperature for up to two weeks.

This Orange Blossom Turkish Delight recipe offers a delicate and aromatic flavor, perfect for citrus and floral enthusiasts alike. Enjoy making and sharing this delightful confection with friends and family!

Blackcurrant Turkish Delight

Ingredients:

- 2 cups blackcurrant juice (freshly squeezed or from concentrate)
- 2 cups granulated sugar
- 1 cup water
- 1 tablespoon lemon juice
- 1/2 cup cornstarch
- 1 1/2 cups water
- Powdered sugar, for dusting

Instructions:

1. Grease a square baking dish (about 8x8 inches) with oil and line it with parchment paper.
2. In a medium saucepan, combine the blackcurrant juice, granulated sugar, 1 cup of water, and lemon juice. Stir over medium heat until the sugar dissolves completely.
3. In a separate bowl, mix the cornstarch with 1 1/2 cups of water until smooth and there are no lumps.
4. Gradually pour the cornstarch mixture into the saucepan with the blackcurrant syrup, stirring constantly to prevent lumps.
5. Cook the mixture over medium heat, stirring frequently, until it thickens and starts to pull away from the sides of the pan. This usually takes about 15-20 minutes.
6. Continue to cook the mixture for another 5-10 minutes until it becomes very thick and glossy.
7. Immediately pour the hot mixture into the prepared baking dish. Smooth out the top with an oiled spatula or spoon.
8. Allow the Turkish delight to cool at room temperature for several hours, until it is completely set and firm.

9. Once set, lift the Blackcurrant Turkish delight out of the baking dish using the parchment paper. Place it on a cutting board and cut it into small squares or rectangles using a sharp knife.
10. Dust the cut pieces with powdered sugar to prevent them from sticking together.
11. Your Blackcurrant Turkish Delight is now ready to be enjoyed! Store the pieces in an airtight container at room temperature for up to two weeks.

This Blackcurrant Turkish Delight recipe offers a tart and fruity flavor, perfect for blackcurrant enthusiasts. Enjoy making and sharing this delicious confection with friends and family!

www.ingramcontent.com/pod-product-compliance
Lightning Source LLC
LaVergne TN
LVHW081329060526
838201LV00055B/2542